YOU ARE NOT ALONE:

A Rwandan Memoir

By Verediane Mukagatanazi

Chapbook Press

Schuler Books
2660 28th Street SE
Grand Rapids, MI 49512
(616) 942-7330
www.schulerbooks.com

ISBN 13: 9781936243914
ISBN 10: 1936243911

Library of Congress Control Number: 2014959724

Copyright © 2014, Verediane Mukagatanazi

All rights reserved. No part of this book may be reproduced in any form without express permission of the copyright holder.

Printed in the United States by Chapbook Press.

To my daughters:

Joy
Sandrine
Sabine
&
Grace

Acknowledgments

To Dr. Marguerite Stiefbold,

When you suggested, during one of our family therapy sessions, that I wrote my story (which is also the story of my family), you had pressed on the right button. It was difficult at times, but in the end, it was liberating. You are the best family therapist ever!

To Grace Twagilimana,

When you suggested a chronological order for my story, you had made my dream of writing a good story come true. You are so clever and you have an amazing insight on books and everything else.

To Sandrine Zilikana,

Your technological knowledge was a beautiful complement to my old traditional powers. You were near when I needed your help.

To Randy Fletcher,

I appreciate every effort you put into the realization of this book. From manuscript to printing and beyond, your commitment and dedication were without measure...

Thank you all!

Contents

Prologue 15
Chapter One: Childhood memories 17
Chapter Two: Education 25
Chapter Three: A slow-cooker relationship 33
Chapter Four: Together and apart 41
Chapter Five: "Where there is love, there are always miracles." 45
Chapter Six: A city on fire 49
Chapter Seven: No safety for me anywhere 53
Chapter Eight: One presidential aircraft, hundreds of thousands dead 57
Chapter Nine: Away 63
Chapter Ten: My cultural journey in America 68
Chapter Eleven: You are not alone 78
Epilogue 82

Author and her husband, 2000, and Verediane's wreath of yarn.

Author's Note

This is my story. It is also the story of my family. It is supposed to be a true story, even though a few details may not have been very well remembered. I appreciate your understanding.

A Note From Sabine

I wish I knew what to write that would be worthy of sharing space in a book written by my mother. My brain keeps drawing a blank.

Do I write about how little we know each other and how desperately I want for us to be known? And maybe I don't give us enough credit. You've known me from the time I was born and lived with me every day until I left home for IMSA. I'm sure there are things you've observed in me before I realized them in myself, prayers you've prayed that helped make me the woman that I am, and private journals you've read without my permission...but do you know why I ran the marathon two years ago and why I'm doing the triathlon this year? Do you know that fulfilling those dreams makes me more confident to make other dreams come true—like buying a motorcycle and exploring the whole country because I've only been to six of the fifty States? Or hiking the Appalachian or Pacific Crest Trail despite the blisters and body aches and solitude because I might learn something significant about myself or God or love that's worth knowing? And do you know that these dreams frighten me but the prospect of living without dreams frightens me even more?

There's a quote that goes, "He who is not everyday conquering some fear has not learned the secret of life." -Ralph Waldo Emerson. Isn't that true?

And I wonder what you dream about and whether there are dreams you've had but haven't had the courage/time/opportunity to express. When/how will you choose to express them? And what are you afraid of?

I think I'm most afraid of being alone. But when you seek the antidote for loneliness in other people, you will always be lonely because no one can hear your thoughts or see your dreams like you can. There's a limit to how well we can know one another. That's why I appreciate your daily mindful practice of watching the day end as night creeps in in a dark room by yourself while you massage your muscles. What a simple way to honor yourself and give witness to whatever's going on inside you. If no one else knows you in that moment, at least you know yourself.

I think it's hard to really see people. It takes practice and intention. I hope your book helps me see who you are, not just as a mother but as an individual, as a woman.

I don't know what to write for your book so I hope this is enough. And even though we live different lives in different places, I hope this is the start of a journey that goes beyond these pages.

Foreword

How does one survive the trauma of war - bombings, shootings, killings, rapes? In this day and age, the U.S. media reports the struggles and despair of our own troops who have witnessed the atrocities of war as they attempt to find some meaning in the horrors they have experienced. As a civilian caught in the ravages of war, how does a woman alone with three babies, hiding and moving from place to place for six years, survive and protect her children? This is the story of a young mother during the Rwandan genocide. It is a story of faith, love, courage, and tenacity, as she awakens one morning to war while her husband is studying in the United States trying to make a better life for his family. In telling this story twenty years later, healing from this terrifying experience continues, as fear lessens its grip. This story of courage is a testament to this mother and wife and her decision to love and protect those near to her heart, no matter the cost. Her story of resilience lives on today with her decision to move beyond the frightening past using her gift of faith, her family traditions of nurturing and perseverance, and her poetic writing to recount what would be for anyone, a horrifying experience.

Dr. Marguerite Stiefbold
Licensed Marriage and Family Therapist

PROLOGUE

It was supposed to be a normal day. I was supposed to go about my day, doing normal things, the usual way. And I was ready. Ready to go to school where I was a teacher. The school was about a mile away from my house. I could see the school from my house, which was a few steps away from a military camp.

I had just kissed my babies goodbye, given orders to the housekeeper and I was out the door. That's when I heard loud noises and saw lightnings in the sky. Something terrible had just begun. I was not familiar with the sounds of the guns, grenades, mortar, and bombs…

I quickly retreated back to the house and locked the door. I could see through the window people running in all directions. I could hear them scream. It was chaos. It was scary. What was going on?

The City was under attack. The rebels were in town. The armed forces were fighting the rebels. The military camp next to my house was certainly a target. I was in a war zone. What was I going to do with three babies, all under three years old?

Under the bed with the babies, I could hear glasses from the windows falling. It seemed the house was shaking. In any moment, our lives would be over. The noises, the sounds of the artillery were too much to bear.

Then the phone rang.

CHAPTER ONE:
Childhood Memories

I was born in the country, far away from the city. I occasionally went to the city with my father when I was a child. We lived off the land. We grew our own food and raised a few animals. I fetched for water from the well, collected firewood and walked to school every day of the week.

One day, I went to fetch for water. Rain and hail came down on me as I walked back home carrying a pot (actually a saucepan) of water on my head. I started running towards home as the water and the rain poured on me. When I got home, there was very little water left in the pot. My mother told me I should have covered my head with the pot for a little protection. I was about six years old.

A special tree whose sap coagulated on the bark provided a special treat. Kids removed the gooey stuff from the bark of the tree and popped it in their mouth. I was no different then. It possibly was my very first candy. It tasted somewhat sweet and sour, but mostly sweet.

I certainly gathered juicy wild berries on my way back home from school. The vines had thorns but they did not stop me from collecting handfuls of yummy berries. And I knew which ones tasted best: the darker ones!

Nature provided wild mushrooms as well. We did not grow mushrooms at all. They grew on their own and were seasonal. People knew when mushrooms would pop up from the ground. They would go check the area around the time the mushrooms usually appeared. Then it was by word of mouth among neighbors that they learned of the upcoming event: the harvest of mushrooms! They were the best mushrooms I ever ate in my life.

Food was prepared on open fire. You could roast sweet corn. You could roast meat the same way you roast marshmallows. Potatoes, sweet potatoes and other root vegetables could be roasted in hot ashes.

There was no baking. So I had neither cakes nor cookies as a kid. If Santa Claus had come to visit, He would have been offered sweet potatoes. My folks prepared food as it is done on the top of the stove. It was mostly cooked in water, since we did not use oil. No fries! Very little salt or no salt at all! No use of sugar!

Meat was very rare. In fact there was a name for meat, "Imbonekarimwe," a compound word that means, "what you see (have) once!" Once a year? Once a month? Once a week? I have no idea! But certainly not once a day! Our animals were raised for the market. They were a source of income. You were considered rich among neighbors if you owned more animals, more children and a large plantation of bananas. So the animals were not for us to eat. We had beans, legumes and sometimes eggs and milk for protein.

Having meat was a memorable experience. My mother would cook the meat for hours. It was cooked in water, which would turn into broth. When the meat was ready, (my mother knew it, not the thermometer!) it was separated from the broth. Then we would gather to eat, sitting around in a circle. There would be bread (umutsima) cooked in water!

My father would share the meat among us all children. He would call each one of us by his or her name, and he would hand us a piece of meat. We had seconds and sometimes thirds.

We sat on a mat layed on the floor. It was actually considered rude for someone to eat while standing up! We ate with our hands, not with forks and knives. My mother would pour the broth in a large bowl, which we would pass around after a sip or two. Never mind the germs! We possibly did not know of their existence. Besides, we were just sharing a meal as a family, making memories.

It was plain organic meat. The broth was excellent having had spices added to it. I never tasted better meat anywhere else! Was it because it was rare that it tasted so good? Was it the organic flavor? Or simply the environment itself?

Dinner time? Not exactly at 6:00 pm. There was no clock ticking! Maybe when the sun disappeared behind the horizon! Anyway, it was dinnertime when food was ready. We did not have snacks between meals. Therefore, everybody was ready to eat at the same time. We shared food.

A practice that seemed to come naturally was when the older kids left some food on the plate for the younger ones. We all ate from the same plate! The food was not always enough but it was shared. It was almost always the same food with not much variety. That probably kept food allergies away! I would say my life was quite the same everyday. Nothing new to try, not much of excitement!

One thing that brought excitement in my childhood was a road construction. The road passed right through our property and we had to move quickly. My father put up a small house and we moved in before it was completed. We would see stars above us as we lay down to sleep.

I got to see people who were different from me. Their skin, their hair were not the same as mine. They were Italians who oversaw the road construction. Their headquarters were just about three miles away from my house. We called them "Abazungu" (Whites).

I saw a bulldozer moving earth for the very first time. I would basically imitate the movement with my hand. So did many other kids my age. Watching the machinery at work, hearing the explosions of the rocks bursting, was like watching an action movie.

The excitement was for everyone. My father got his very first and last paying job. He bought new clothes for my mother and for us kids. My mother kept her new clothes neatly folded in her wooden suitcase (no closet!), clothes she would wear only to church on Sunday.

My father tasted and drank whiskey for the first time in his life and he would talk about that experience for the rest of his life! He got the drink from an Italian friend. When he got home after work, he went straight to bed, which was very unusual. We thought he was sick but he was not.

The road building in this remote area did not go without a price. People got hurt and people got killed. My father got injured while riding in a car on the job. He was in the hospital for two days. A huge stone that rolled all the way down the hill to where she was digging sweet potatoes from the ground killed a neighbor. She got knocked down by the stone and died instantly. There were other horrible stories but I did not witness those.

The road construction was absolutely a need there. Once completed, it connected two nations: Rwanda and Uganda, a neighboring country in the North; from the Capital City (Kigali) all the way to the Northern border (Gatuna). It was basically one of the best roads in the country. And I might as well say I was no longer in the middle of nowhere! The road would serve me a great deal as I traveled to and from my schools.

As a child, it was very common for a family to sit around a burning fire, whether food was cooking or not. That was our way to warm ourselves up. There were lots of stories to tell and lots of stories to listen to. Some stories warmed up our hearts; some others scared us to death. There were lessons to be learned from the stories. Some taught us how to live, some others taught us how to love and mind our manners.

A practice I remember as a child was about the birth of a baby in the family. It concerned the naming of the newborn. Children in the neighborhood were invited to gather at the house where the baby was born. They all sat on a mat in a large circle and plates of food were placed in the center for kids to enjoy. Afterwards, the baby was placed in every child's lap. He or she thought of a name to give to the newborn. They took turns doing so. And of course, a grown-up assisted them! You didn't want them to drop the baby! The practice was disappearing as I was growing up.

But looking back, I think it was a nice way to have kids come together. Most gatherings were for grown-ups who gathered around alcohol drinks. So, that was one of the rare occasions when kids had an opportunity to express themselves in a "formal" situation. And besides, in a place where Birthdays celebrations are not a popular event, the practice could be considered a birth day celebration. After all, we are born only once!

My folks were hand-makers. Almost everything used around the house was handmade. The needed material was nature provided. Sometimes, you found it close to home, sometimes, you walked far to find it.

There were large built-in storages (Ibigega) to contain the grain or other crops. Girls made mats that served as blankets or for people to sit on. They also made baskets that served as storages as well. They made wreaths to decorate the house. Boys made a kind of basket (igitebo) that was used to carry sweet potatoes, potatoes, and other harvest.

Some people worked iron to make hoes (amasuka) that were used in digging. These were absolutely a basic need for farmers since there was no machinery. They also made spears and machetes.

There were potters who worked with clay to make pots, large and small. Pots were used in storing water, cooking and carrying alcoholic drinks to friends and relatives. In many ceremonial events like weddings, alcoholic drinks from bananas and sorghum were poured in a huge pot and people gathered around the pot to drink, using tall straws. Out of respect, you were supposed to get on your knees while drinking. There was somebody to make sure everybody got his or her turn. Children could be excused from drinking while standing up. They would not reach the tip of the straws anyway!

Sorghum was quite a popular crop. Not only did it provide the grain for food and alcohol usage, it also provided the material used to build fences around the house. The fence was necessary, especially if you owned animals. Once the fence was built, there was an entrance that was blocked at night, when the animals were gathered inside. There was no gate! The entrance was blocked by a large pile of logs, (imyugariro) all the way up!

The blocking of the entrance seemed to indicate curfew! You were late if you came home afterwards. Girls especially were supposed to be home before the entrance was blocked. If you came late, you would need to call somebody out loud to remove some of the logs so you could climb over the rest. You could hurt yourself doing so. I remember my father having a fight with my older sister for coming home late. So you did not want to end up in that kind of situation.

Once my father blocked the entrance as soon as he got home from work. He had gotten a job with the road construction. The animals were still grazing under a beautiful sunset. My father went straight to bed. He did not notice at all how early it was. He had had a drink of whiskey for the first time in his life. My brother had to unblock the entrance for the animals to get inside, while my father slept soundly in bed. We did not hear of anything until the next day! My father could not even remember how he got home. He could not recall what he did the previous night!

My parents had a good relationship, but I hated it when they had drinks of alcohol, because there were more chances of a fight. I grew up in a monogamous family where divorce was not talked about. You married for better or for worse! Some of my neighbors were polygamous; with two or more wives and each wife having her own house.

Sometimes, my parents separated after a fight when I was little. In those few cases, my mother would go back to her parents. But my father would go get her back soon afterwards. My mother told me that when I was a baby, she went to her parents taking me with her since I was nursing. I got sick there and she had to return home to my father on her own without him going to look for her. It was possibly the last time she was in that kind of situation. Later, they would fight but she would not go anywhere.

Many marriages were arranged. That meant people married without knowing each other. I would think it was the case for my parents, considering how far my mother came from. Also, that was way back when arranged marriages were the norm.

My siblings who got married knew their 'fiancé'. My aunt

introduced this one guy to my sister but they got to know each other before they married. He would come to visit our family sometimes. The others met their fiancé on their own. Either they lived nearby or had met in the primary school. They mostly married young since they did not get to further their education.

More memories from my childhood are of:

Dust. Smoke. Dirt. Harvest. Peace. Calm. Lovely singing birds.

Beautiful sunset.

Rain...heavy rain.

Grazing cows.

Peeping chicks.

Working farmers.

Talking neighbors.

Newborn calves.

Fields of corn.

A few flowers.

Large plantations of bananas.

A view of mountains.

Lots of trails.

Small houses.

Stars at night.

Sunshine

Moon

Darkness

Silence...

CHAPTER TWO:
Education

There were six years of primary school, followed by secondary school which was divided into two sections: three years of high school and three or four years of specific training. After this specific training, you worked for two years before going to college. There have been reforms through the years. You passed a standardized test in order to go to high school and you paid school fees there. There were three breaks in a school year: Christmas break, Easter break and summer break.

My course of education took longer than it should have. It was not a straight path like the one above.

Education was not for everybody where I grew up. Boys guarded cows and goats while girls did house work. Most girls, in particular, did not attend school. They did cooking, cleaning, made mats and baskets as they waited to grow up just enough to produce children.

In my family, everybody got a chance to go to school but not beyond primary school. My oldest brother, the first child in the family, passed the test to attend high school but my parents could not afford to pay school fees. One sister dropped out of school in third grade, after being slapped hard by a teacher. I was the only one in a family of nine children to graduate from college.

From first to fourth grade, I attended a primary school that was a little close to home. But fifth and sixth grades were a little too far away. Most often I had to fetch for water before going to school.

In those days, the principal whipped the legs of students who were late for school with a stick. That was the routine. I happened to be a teacher's favorite. He would call my name, as I waited in line to be beaten up by the principal. He would signal me to go to him and would tell me to go in the classroom. That way, the principal would not get me. It became a habit. Each time I was late, I knew I was safe in the hands of my teacher. I was possibly the smallest but I was also intelligent.

The same teacher directed the choir that sang in church during the Sunday service. I was a member of the choir. I loved all the Christian songs in my native language. To me, my sixth grade teacher was like a father…

In the summer after finishing Primary School, a teacher who was related to my mother came home with good news! I was on the list of those who had been selected to attend secondary school. I was very much excited but I also worried that my parents would not be able to afford the school fees. Fortunately, my father had saved some money from the road construction job and he would sell a few cows in order to pay for my education.

As said by Allan Bloom, "Education is the movement from darkness to light," my life was about to change. I was going to a boarding school for girls, led by nuns—a Catholic school. I would wear uniform there, so clothes were not a big deal. I would wear shoes for the first time and by shoes, I mean slippers. I would have a tube of toothpaste and a toothbrush. Soap and some lotion for skin care. I would buy pens and pencils, pairs of underwear too. I would carry with me some notebooks and a nightgown. A towel, blanket and sheets were also necessary. For the first time, I would sleep on a bed with mattress on it!

The transition from home to my boarding school went quite smoothly. The school owned a large plantation of bananas. There were gardens of vegetables. There was even a compost bin. We had chores every morning before classes. We sometimes went to cut hay to fill up our mattresses. We slept on bunk beds in a large dormitory.

I loved being in the classroom. We studied almost everything, from mathematics and sciences to sewing and cooking. My favorite subject was French. My French teacher was incredible. She had studied in France. She wore pants at all times. That was her style. She had short hair. She was unique. She was special. She carried herself with confidence. I might as well say I wanted to be like her, and I loved French so much. She was the first woman I saw wearing pants!

I happened to have the best handwriting around that age of thirteen to fifteen. Maybe later on, too. But at this particular time, I was chosen to do the class journal. It had to be done neatly and there was only one for each class. I did that for three consecutive years...

The teachers usually wrote notes on the blackboard while students took them in their notebooks. One particular teacher would leave his notes and I would write them on the blackboard for the rest of the students. I would do that during study time that we had every night before bed. The teacher admired my handwriting and I loved being in charge.

He rewarded me with a big plain notebook, my very first present ever! The teacher got a new job and left the school but even afterwards, he wrote me a letter advising me on how to prepare for the up-coming test: I was in the third year of High School. I would have to pass the test in order to go on with my education. I took his advice to heart, I studied hard like he wanted me to and passed the test. He was like a father to me!

I was quite stubborn. One day, one of my friends was sick in bed. The dormitory was locked. I climbed the window and went through to keep my friend company. As I was coming out the same way, I was caught by the principal who punished me by making me stay right there in the window for an hour so everybody could see me—including my teachers. It happened during a bathroom break so I missed a whole hour of class. It might have been humiliating but I don't think I was. I possibly considered myself as being on stage.

Another day, it was study time. We all sat in the classroom every night before bed to study. The principal would pass by the classroom, peering through the window to see how studious we were. She did not need to come inside at all. Sometimes we would not know she was there unless she came closer to the window. Otherwise, with the lights on inside the classroom, and the outside being dark, the principal could see us without us noticing her.

One day, instead of being in my seat, I was in front of the class, sitting in the corner near the door. I was not studying. I was fixing my friend's slippers, with a thread and a needle. As the principal stood outside by the window, the other students were staring in my direction, sort of laughing. This made the principal suspicious or maybe curious. She opened the door, which could not go all the way because I was blocking it. She peered behind the door to find me, sitting and repairing slippers. This time she did not punish me. She told me to regain my seat.

I spoke when I was supposed to be quiet. And when I spoke, I was loud; I wanted everybody to hear me. My friends called me "Véridique," French for "who tells the truth." The nickname almost sounded like my real name, Verediane. I loved being called "Véridique." We all went by our nicknames. One girl's nickname was "mouchette," French for "a tiny fly." I had so many friends there. You could say I was a popular girl. I fixed everybody's hair but mine…

One day, I was asked to bring my father to school. That meant writing a letter to my father which would take more than two weeks to get to him. But upon receiving my letter, my father reported immediately to the school. He might have thought I had been sick since he did not know why he was needed there.

I was then called in the office where my father was waiting for me. He gave me a hug and saw I was all right. The principal then told him I was stubborn. The nuns offered him an alcoholic drink made from bananas. He would say later that the drink was the best of its kind he ever had. He might have been very thirsty though, because he had made such a long trip on foot to get to my school. After all, my father made that sort of drink very often. But he was impressed that the nuns there made it better than him. He might have been too shy to ask for the recipe.

We had some sort of entertainment on Saturdays after classes. There was a loud speaker and we danced to loud music in front of the dormitory. That was kind of a treat to us.

There was also a high school for boys who were our neighbors. Some girls had pen pals there. One day, we were invited there for a dance. We were all supposed to be on the dance floor, no exception. Some girls were too shy to dance, but the principal would find partners for them. She wanted every girl to have a partner. Later she quit the monastery to get married…

After three years of secondary school, my dream was to become a secretary somewhere in a city. So I attended another boarding school for girls, for the secretary program. The program normally lasted three years. But I was out after two years. I had failed. I was lucky enough to transfer to a teaching training. That meant a new beginning. It would take four years in another boarding school.

My new boarding school was very far from home. I was crossing the entire country to get there. It was located near a lake; the first time I saw a large body of water up close. In fact we fetched for water there one time. My training in this school was going to be extraordinary...

It was the first time there was ever a bookcase in my classroom! We had a reading hour on Sunday afternoons. I loved books. I loved all of them, but mostly autobiographies. One, in particular, was written by Peter Abrahams, "Je ne suis pas un homme libre." French for "I am not a free man." It was a South African autobiography. I loved true stories...

My French teacher there was excellent. I loved this particular project that was related to reading. It also involved lots of writing. It was an individual project. Each student selected a book to work on. We studied the characters in the book, the language itself, the vocabulary. We did research about the author of the book and we did the summary of the story. It wasn't just reading a book. It was digging into it. I was amazed at how much I could learn from a book. I loved that project so much.

The teacher wore white pants and a white shirt at all times! Neat! With a tie! Something not so popular there. He also wore glasses. Back there, you were considered "intelligent" if you wore them. My French teacher extended his neatness to our notebooks. He collected all of them regularly to see how they were maintained. He graded us and I scored high. Possibly the only teacher I saw doing that. He had truly mastered the French language. No doubt, he was an inspiration for me.

My trips to that school were very difficult. They included many stops, dusty roads and muddy in the rainy season. One time, Augustin accompanied me on one of those trips halfway. He was a college student. It was a great feeling sitting with him on the bus. I got into accidents a couple times but I did not get hurt. It took me about two days to travel to my school. During the teaching training, I developed a good taste for art. I remember one time, it was Christmas Celebration and the principal, who was white, asked me to sketch the nativity scene on the blackboard in the large room where the celebration was to be held. I had a few compliments about my work! I also wrote poetry. Inspiration seemed to come from everywhere. It seemed very easy and simple to write my poems.

I loved my teaching training. After graduation, I would have to work for two years before going to college...

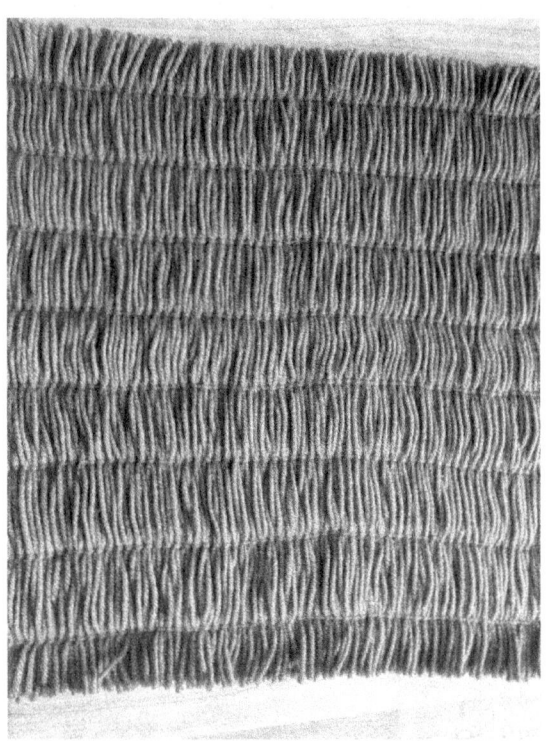

An out of yarn handmade mat.

CHAPTER THREE:
A Slow-cooker relationship

After graduating from high school, I worked as a teacher at a local grade school, the same school I attended as a child, but this time it had grades from first to seventh. I was then able to earn a little money that was used to build a larger house for my parents. I felt so happy when it was completed and they moved in. It was a simple way of showing my gratitude but I also thought my destiny was not to be with them forever. I was looking forward into the future…

A future with Augustin. A handsome young man I had come to love. I don't remember the first time I met him. I must have been fourteen or fifteen years old.

His family lived about five miles away from mine. We did not have phones nor cars. We lived very simple lives in the middle of the country; away from the city. To see someone or talk to someone, you walked to them. Augustin would often come at my house. He became a familiar face in my household. Everybody liked him. He was a brother to me.

One day I was home having a headache and he brought me a few pills. They were green and tasted like candy. I felt much better. Another day, I was at school teaching. He was home on break from college. A terrible storm came down just as it was time to go home. I was stuck in the classroom. I looked out the window and there stood

Augustin! He had brought me an umbrella.

We walked together in the heavy rain. Me holding him by the waist, him by my shoulders. On our way home, we met my brother who was also bringing me an umbrella. Augustin walked with us all the way to my family. In fact, he had a sleepover. His first sleepover at my house.

For years we had a brother-sister kind of relationship enjoying simple pleasures: walking together, watching a sunset, listening to music on the radio. He had given me the radio as his very first present! He also loved books. We read some together. His family was pretty much educated, especially the boys. We did not have television nor computers. We did not have electricity at all. But we were happy. We were nurturing our relationship the most natural way possible.

One summer, we took a long trip together. I was going to retrieve my diploma from the school where I did teaching training. I would eventually introduce him to the nuns as "my uncle". The trip included spending nights in the hotel, the view of the lake, long rides on the bus, eating in restaurants, a ride on a boat and some flirtations.

The lake was beautiful. The sunset was very bright. It was calm. It was almost night. The only sound was the sound of the lake. It seemed we were the only people on Earth. Just two of us. He gave me a kiss. The moment was magical. We were in love...

> *Love is real. Love is true.*
> *Love is for everyone.*
> *Love is a seed, sow it.*
> *Love is a fruit, pick it.*
> *Love is a jewel, wear it.*
> *Love is a sunset, watch it.*

Love is pure water, drink it.
Love is kind, be kind.
Love is a feeling, feel it.
Love is tender, nurture it.
Love is unique, accept it.
Love is beautiful, admire it.
Love is a flower, smell it.
Love is cuddly, touch it.
Love is a fire, but fear not...

Fear is the enemy of love. Expressing love between sexes in some cultures can be a challenge. It was a routine for me to escort Augustin whenever he came to visit my family. There was this particular spot, halfway between his home and mine, where we would stop for a while, and sometimes longer than an hour, before we could separate from each other. One day as we kissed good-bye right there at our favorite spot, a small rock landed next to us. Somebody had thrown a rock at us as if to say, "I see you!"

Of course we were seen very often together. And we had nothing to hide.

One old man, in particular, caught our attention. He was deaf from birth. And his name summed it all up: "Kiragi" for "deaf". We passed by his house almost every day. He eventually saw there was opportunity to talk to us, to express himself in his own way. We were never in a hurry. We walked slowly, hand in hand, smiling and sometimes laughing. We were young, happy and in love...

The old man would sit outside his house waiting for us. He spoke sign language. His very own sign language, not the American sign language. He had never been anywhere to study that. Those familiar with him could understand his sign language. As we spent time with him, we eventually became familiar with his language. He spoke the language of love to us. That's what we inspired him to talk about. And that's what we could understand from the kind of person he was.

The old man was extremely unique. He lived alone. He had never been married. He had no children. You would think he was lonely, especially because he was also deaf. But as soon as he saw us, his face lightened up with a huge smile. He appeared younger, full of life. He seemed to have rehearsed his sign language, because he would go on and on. He was quite an entertainer and in return, we offered him company for a while...

We might have been unique as well. Therefore, we connected deeply with the old man who spoke the language of love, the only language we could understand... Mark Twain said, "Kindness is the language which the deaf can hear and the blind can see." I would say the same is true about love.

As a girl, visiting a young man and his family was not popular in my culture. But as many years passed and our relationship blossomed, I got to visit Augustin at his family's home. I became familiar with everybody there, especially with his sister whose name, Verediane, is mine. Another sister's name, Venantie, matched the name of my younger sister. It seemed the connection between our families was quite natural.

Augustin and I walked to see some of my other relatives. We got to visit my uncle's family whose wife was my godmother. We took a taxi to visit his brother's family who lived in the Capital City. I can say that not only did we know each other but we also knew each other's family quite well.

Sex before marriage was forbidden. In fact, the subject was avoided all together. Augustin and I spent lovely moments together but he respected my values. He was careful about everything.

About eight years into our relationship, it seemed a moment of change had come. Augustin was then working on his master's degree at University. I was a teacher living home with my parents. We saw each other when he came for break so there were times we missed each other. One day, he came home to see me and invited me to his house for the next day. I was used to going to his house. He also told me that it was time to consider a more intimate relationship with him.

When I got to his house the next day, he invited me into his bedroom, which was not our usual place to sit. I hesitated and refused to join him. When his sister went to find him in his room, he wrote on a tiny piece of paper that he needed me. And as his sister handed me the tiny note, she also commented that her brother was a little difficult.

I finally went into his room because I loved him. When he wanted to do more intimate stuff after a few kisses, I was scared. And he did not know how to go about it. We had failed. The same way we had failed when we tried to kiss for the first time. He had then asked me afterwards, "Tu ne sais pas embrasser?" (You don't know how to kiss?)

This time though, we were even more disappointed because what he saw was lack of love. He thought I had pushed him away. He thought I had rejected him. He thought that maybe I was not normal. I had tortured him with my presence and he was never ever going to see me again...

Back home I was in pain. Everybody could see I was the most miserable person on Earth. I couldn't hide my tears. I was going through a tough crisis. I was being hit pretty bad. I considered we had come a very long way, crossing so many barriers. I could not understand myself, I was in a total confusion. The break-up time was going to be very difficult.

I wrote a letter to Augustin and gave it to my younger sister to deliver to him. When she got there, Augustin was burning a big pile of letters. When my sister came back and told me what she saw, I was mortified. I was devastated. I was heart-broken. I wanted to disappear from the face of the Earth. I wanted to die.

Augustin's break was over. It had been a disaster. It had been a painful break-up, and he was back at the University. That was the first time in my life I felt so lonely. It was also the first time I learned how it feels to love someone. "The way to love anything is to realize that it might be lost." (GK Chesterton)

I came to realize Augustin was very special. He was actually gentle. He was handsome. He was intelligent. He had been patient with me through so many years. Augustin was caring and most importantly, loving. I loved everything about him. I knew the change was about me; not about him or maybe just a little. I had been safe with him for long. He had been a brother to me. He did not want me to be in any trouble. We had slept in the same house. We had slept in the same room. We had slept in the same bed. He had shown so much respect for me. He had endured so much. I was determined to fully open my heart to him. He deserved the best.

Back at the University, Augustin wrote me a letter. He had not given up on me. He wanted me to visit him on campus.

Even as I decided to go to him, I went with my younger brother who ended up finding another roommate, a close friend of Augustin. That night was supposed to be special for the two of us. After all, we knew what we were up to.

We faced almost the same difficulties as the previous time he tried more intimacy. This time though, it was more of physical pain than being scared. So we couldn't get anywhere and we went to sleep a little disappointed.

I knew I was normal. Augustin could not get it. We both seemed to be in unknown territory. Early in the morning, I took a shower, preparing myself to return home. Back from the shower, I found Augustin was still in bed. I could tell he desired me no matter the circumstances. He did not want me to leave so soon. He kissed me tenderly. We cuddled. I was back in bed. This time things went smoothly. I would say the hardest part had been done! We had made love as well as memories....

The break-up was a turning point in our relationship. It was a wake-up call for me. I needed to break free from whatever was holding me back. I needed to move forward. I needed to understand the true meaning of love. I needed to make a fair decision. I needed to wake up from my dreams. After all, Augustin was not my brother. He was neither my uncle, nor my father either. He had represented all of those in some ways, but Augustin was this powerful man with a powerful heart...

In matters of love, follow your heart.
You may seek advice, but the decision
   is always yours to make.
No one can feel love for you.
No one can teach you how to love.
No one can translate love for you.
Because love is deeper than you think
And its home is your very own heart.
There are no limits, no barriers to love.
A break-up can be painful,

But if you are meant to be together,
It won't be long until the green
light appears again.
Love is stronger than cultural
demands, because: love is liberation
Love is incredible
Love is powerful
Love is freedom.

CHAPTER FOUR:
Together and apart

Augustin and I dated intensively after the break-up. We had crossed the bridge hand in hand. We were safe on the other side. We were free.

In the summer of 1986, we had a civil wedding. That meant that we were officially married. I was also starting college in the fall that same year. Augustin was done with his master's degree and he was going to be a high school teacher. He transferred from one school to another to get closer to me. The new school was about thirty miles from campus. I would live on campus but we would spend weekends together at his apartment.

I had the opportunity to have a ride every weekend from campus to the school where Augustin was the teacher. We made lots of memories during this period of time; memories that would carry us through thick and thin.

Augustin would visit me on campus whenever he thought of coming. He became a familiar face there and the guys called him "beau-frère" (brother-in-law). Once again, I was safe. No one was going to bother me! I belonged to somebody! And all these guys were my brothers!

One Friday afternoon, I tried to nap after classes but I found myself thinking about Augustin. I told my roommate I was going to see him. She noticed the change in my usual schedule. But we did not have any exam that weekend. She just couldn't understand how crazy I was about Augustin.

It was getting late and this time I had no ride, so I took a taxi to Augustin's apartment. He had no idea I was coming. I entered his apartment and sat in the living room, wondering how he was going to react to my surprise. He was in his bedroom possibly daydreaming about the weekend. He asked who was there. I was quiet. Then he came and found me. He pulled me gently closer to his chest. I could feel his heart beating really fast. And so was mine!

One time as I stood with Augustin by the side of the road, waiting for a ride, a middle-aged man passed by us. He looked carefully at us and concluded that I perfectly resembled my father. And by "my father" he meant Augustin. We were married. We did not say a word! There is something special about being short and having short hair: you are forever young!

Our religious ceremony was in August, 1988. It was Saturday and Augustin had just received a promotion in his job career. He was no longer a teacher. He was starting the new job on Monday, following our wedding. His best man commented that I had brought luck to Augustin, referring to the promotion.

The new job meant Augustin was going to move to this northern city, which was actually our birthplace, and I still had work to do on campus. The distance was going to be longer between us. We were in two different cities. I was also pregnant with our first child.

I eventually moved out of campus and found an apartment in town as my due date approached. Augustin managed pretty well to come to see me every weekend as he adjusted to his new job. One weekend as he was visiting me, I thought I was in labor. So we went to the hospital but the nurse suggested to go back home and wait. She thought it was too early. It was Monday and Augustin had to return to his job.

By the evening, I was in real labor and went back to the hospital. I called Augustin who reported to the hospital. He was there on Tuesday, when our beautiful baby girl arrived about 6:40pm. It was November 22, 1988. She was named Joy Maliza.

Maliza means the very first-born in a family. We joined Augustin soon after the baby was born. I was also graduating from college. We were going to settle in this small town and raise our family. But once again things were about to change.

At the end of 1989, Augustin learned he had to get in the USA to begin a six-year doctorate program. It was a great opportunity for him and for our family. After all, we lived in an underdeveloped country where there was no such opportunity. You couldn't get anything beyond a master's degree. By the time he left for the States, I was about seven months pregnant again…

I felt very sad at the airport after his good bye kiss as his flight was about to take off. But deep within I knew it was the right thing to do. I knew that we had built a strong relationship. We trusted one another. The connection between us was real and special. We would keep in touch, writing tons of letters, and a phone call once in a while. We also had a few good friends in this small town and I would not feel much loneliness. I had gotten a job as a French teacher in a private high school close to home. We were going to be ok. We also hoped to be reunited as a family in the States maybe after a certain period of time…

Verediane's sailing away painting.

CHAPTER FIVE:
"Where there is love, there are always miracles"
– Willa Cather

So, I was in bed by myself. I woke up around mid-night to realize I was in labor. I took a quick shower and called my neighbors: a very nice couple who had become our friends and lived just across the street from us. They had six children.

They took me to the hospital in that night. In the hospital, the doctors did not come to work until 8:00am, the nurses were the ones in charge of patients at night. They would check on me but nothing was happening except intense labor. They could not understand why the baby was not coming when the waters had broken. But there was nothing else they could do but wait until the arrival of the doctors.

The doctor finally came. I must have been the first patient he saw that morning. After checking on me, he told the nurses to get me ready for caesarean. There were complications and this was an emergency. It was a relief for me to hear the doctor's decision; even if I did not know what to expect of the operation.

In the operating room, things went smoothly. Two beautiful baby girls were born that morning of February 6,1990. A close friend called Augustin in the States to let him know of the arrival of the twin girls. He would call me once at home after being discharged from the hospital. There was no telephone there! We would also discuss the names of the babies at that time. For now, there are: Gakuru (the oldest) and Gato (the youngest) by only two minutes. I learned later that the complications that led to the surgery were about the two babies coming at the same time. How was that going to happen? A miracle, indeed.

Friends and relatives came to see me in the hospital. Augustin's older brother came with his wife. They lived in the capital city. So, they had taken a long trip to get to me in the hospital. They had four children. He joked by asking where in the world did the twins come from? I had never thought of having twins but I sometimes told Augustin that there were many in there! There was a lot of kicking! It was definitely different from my first pregnancy. The wife said she had always wanted to have twins. When I asked her why, she said she could then have one or two pregnancies, not four! I thought she had a good point...

After our first daughter was born, I told Augustin that we could wait a little longer before having another baby but, he wanted more babies as soon as possible. He said: "No! Not until we have three!"

Well, we had three babies. And the next was not going to come anytime soon afterwards. All done, naturally.

After the twins came in our family, there have been two families on Augustin's side who have delivered twins. They are his younger brother and his nephew. Now we know where in the world they come from!

I had not been in school for almost a month as my due date approached. And when they heard the babies had arrived, a group of students came to see me in the hospital. They surrounded my hospital bed and held the babies. They were so compassionate towards me. They seemed to understand there was an emptiness there to fill; the fact that my husband was overseas instilled some compassion in the hearts of these students. After all, I was just a French teacher to them. I was even new to them. But I felt surrounded by friends, very special friends, not just teenage students.

Once I was back home from the hospital, Augustin called. There were a few friends and family members whom I had invited for a little celebration. Augustin then announced the names of the babies: Zilikana (remember) and Tegura (prepare for the future).

One day my father came for a visit. I had just gotten a letter from Augustin, a letter he had written after receiving the news of the birth of the twins. As I read the letter, I felt very emotional and started to cry. My father looked at the babies and me, and I guessed he understood. I missed Augustin so much as this was a very special moment to share. I wondered if he was ever going to see them any time soon...

Augustin came back for a visit after two years in the States. That was in 1991 and the twins, who were eighteen months old, were able to meet their father for the very first time! As we waited for him at the airport, the girls were running all over the place. He might have been confused a little bit when he saw them. All he knew about them were their photos I tried to send to him sometimes.

We moved to a new house. Our family had grown and Augustin was able to afford a house he found near a military camp with an indoor bathroom and a telephone These amenities weren't common then. The three girls got baptized during this time of his visit. The twins shared the same godparents. They were an incredible couple who assisted me whenever I needed help. At that time, they were moving to the capital city, the husband had found a new job there. We would certainly meet with them again.

Augustin's break was very short but he had met with friends and family. He had moved us and we had had a wonderful time. He had to return to the U.S. He had a lot more to do there. We were looking forward to another special moment when we would be together again.

There was not much hope though, since the country was already at war against the rebels in this northern part of the country. So far, the attacks had been concentrated on the border between Rwanda and Uganda...

CHAPTER SIX:
A city on fire

It was supposed to be a normal day. I was supposed to go about my day, doing normal things, the usual way. And I was ready. Ready to go to school where I was a teacher. The school was about a mile away from my house. I could see the school from my house, which was a few steps away from a military camp.

I had just kissed my babies goodbye, given orders to the housekeeper and I was out the door. That's when I heard loud noises and saw lightnings in the sky. Something terrible had just begun. I was not familiar with the sounds of the guns, grenades, mortar, and bombs...

I quickly retreated back to the house and locked the door. I could see through the window people running in all directions. I could hear them scream. It was chaos. It was scary. What was going on?

The City was under attack. The rebels were in town. The armed forces were fighting the rebels. The military camp next to my house was certainly a target. I was in a war zone. What was I going to do with three babies, all under three years old?

Under the bed with the babies, I could hear glasses from the windows falling. It seemed the house was shaking. In any moment, our lives would be over. The noises, the sounds of the artillery were too much to bear.

Then the phone rang. I hesitated to pull myself from under the bed. But I figured it could be an important call with an important message. I grabbed the receiver and it signaled an international call. It was my husband calling from the United States of America.

The conversation was interrupted. I could not hear what he was saying. The phone had been an important way for both of us to keep in touch. He had gone to pursue his education in the States, a program that was to take him about six years.

It was by phone that he had learned of the birth of our twin girls in February 1990. All he could hear this time were the bombs exploding. He was coming for a break in a week! The day would be Monday. Were we still going to be alive? Were we going to see each other again? Was he going to change his mind?

Sometime in the night, my oldest daughter wanted to use the bathroom. I told her quietly: "Do it right here." I was pointing next to the bed. She screamed, "No!" She was about three years old, when "No" seems to be the answer no matter the circumstances. Even though we had an indoor bathroom, I considered it was best to remain under the bed to avoid any movement. The situation had not changed since morning.

We eventually took a bathroom break, all of us. And that would be it for two full days and nights, because we were neither able to eat nor drink.

It seemed to have been forever. Outside my house lay a body, a young man's body. The intestines had spilled out. Crows were feeding. A picture of a bird pulling a big fat worm from the ground! But this was no picture. This was real life: crows sharing over a human body.

He could have been me. He could have been my child. After all, he was an innocent civilian who worked for a nearby family. He might have been running, trying to save his life. Now, he was gone...

Stop it.
Stop the war.
Stop killing innocent people.
Stop hating each other.
But the war goes on.
More and more senseless acts
*   will be committed.*
One after another...

A group of students showed up at what was left of the door. They came to see what had happened to the babies and me. They had stories of how far they had gone, running. They had seen plain naked people who had been awaken from their sleep by gunshots. Pajamas and nightgowns aren't popular there. Some people are just lucky enough to have what to wear during the day. The students had been on their way to school when the battle began. These were my students and I was simply a French teacher to them. But their compassion for me in a time of crisis was overwhelming… I couldn't even sit down with them and have a nice conversation over a cup of tea. These were times of trouble. The only thing to share was fear. We all worried of what was next. But as I would later read, "A kind and compassionate act is often its own reward." (William J. Bennett)

Another familiar face appeared at the door. He had never been at my house before but I recognize him even in a military uniform. He tells me how lucky we had been, considering the damage done to the house. He tells me also to leave immediately, to go far away from the city. The real battle was about to begin. It was best to leave the city. I did not have any chance to let my husband know we were alive and we were leaving. The phone had died…

When you feel alone
When you think no one cares,
He is real.
He watches over you when you are lost
In fact, you are never lost with him.
The darkness will fall upon you
But the light will shine through.
He holds hands with you when you stumble.
He picks you up when you fall,
He walks by your side.

So we walked and walked miles and many more miles away from the city. Fields of sorghum were such a soothing view. Up and down hills, we walked. Down into the valleys, crossing streams and through the forest, we walked. On our way, we met my brother-in-law who was coming to check on us. I thought it was very nice and extremely courageous of him. We finally arrived at my in-laws as the sun was going down. We were exhausted. We were hungry. We needed a place to lie down and sleep. Maybe forever...

CHAPTER SEVEN:
No safety for me anywhere...

My family visited us at my in-laws. They brought food and milk for the children to drink. I remembered Augustin's phone call. And this was Monday. So, I was waiting for him. No. Not at the airport. Somewhere by the side of the road. In this remote area, with the view of banana plantations and fields of corn, I was waiting for my husband who was to fly from the United States of America...

For hours, I just sat there. My brother-in-law who had accompanied me would ask: "Are you sure he is coming?" After all, we did not talk of the time. We did not talk of the schedule. The phone had died. I might say I was there by the law of faith. I believed he would come. And I refused to think that maybe I did not get the message right. If he was coming, I needed to be waiting for him right there. Otherwise, he would go all the way into the city, which was dangerous at the time. And besides, we were no longer there!

Cars were coming, slowing down for us, looking for passengers. But we were not going anywhere. We were waiting for somebody. Then one car slows down and comes to a stop. My heart was beating faster at this moment. The door opens and out comes Augustin... All the way from America. We hugged. We kissed. But he had yet to meet his daughters and his family before making another move...

We relocated in the Capital City. We lived with his brother's family who had four children. We were desperately looking for our own place to stay since Augustin's break was very short. He wanted us to be settled by the time he was due to return to the States.

So, we found a house; an isolated house compared to the rest of the neighborhood. It had no fence. It was new. We were the first people to rent the house. It seemed not to be completed. But we settled in. It was at a very short distance from the airport. In fact, we all walked with Augustin to the airport as he was going to catch his flight to the U.S. It was the end of 1992.

In the Capital City, we were known as "the displaced of war." And there were so many of us. Those who have come from the northern part of the country which had been ravaged by the war that began in 1990. We were all searching. Searching for jobs, a place to stay and most importantly, searching for safety...

I found a job as a teacher. I would take the bus to work. I would be able to pay for rent and feed my family. We had left everything behind. We had no belongings. We were starting a new life from nothing.

For a while, I thought we were doing fine. My younger brother was living with us while attending a private high school. My oldest daughter was attending the same school as a kindergartner. They would go to school together and come back home together. There was a babysitter to stay home with the twins while I was at work. It seemed we were adapting to life in the Capital City pretty well.

One evening as we prepared ourselves to have dinner, an armed gang of bandits entered our house. They forced the children under the bed. My brother was held under gunpoint. They searched the house, taking whatever they wanted. They asked for money. The babysitter was raped. I was raped. It seemed every attacker had his own task. They wore masks. They were monsters. We were left terrified, terrorized, traumatized. It was the worst of nightmares. It seemed there was no safety for us anywhere. There was a big fat evil everywhere…

A family friend took us in with them. They were the godparents for the twins. They had moved from the northern city where we all used to live. They had come in the Capital City because the husband had found a new job there. They had four children. They lived near a stadium. We stayed with them for a while as I searched for an apartment which I found in the same neighborhood.

It was heart-breaking when I told Augustin on the phone about the attack on us, and what had happened. There were no words to express the truth to someone who was that far away. I wished he was near…

When I confided in a friend that I had told my husband about the rape, she told me she would never had done so if that was her case. Telling the truth is definitely hard to do in some circumstances. But I loved Augustin so much. And I still do. There was nothing that was going to happen to me that he would not get to know. After all, in the words of Mal Pancoast, "Telling someone the truth is a loving act."

The attack on my family could have left us all dead. After all, we were defenseless. Sometimes, it may seem hard to move forward after some experiences in life. But I came to think that there is always a reason to live. So,

In any circumstances,
Don't give up on yourself.
Your family needs you.
Your friends need you.

You are a treasure.
You are beautiful
You are amazing,
You are loving.

You have the right to be angry
You have the right to feel sad
You have the right to feel miserable
But don't give up on yourself.

You are a treasure
You are beautiful
You are amazing
You are loving.

Pick yourself up and move forward.
One step at a time, it won't be so bad
It may be hard to smile again
But the sunshine comes after rain.

We had hoped to be reunited in the States with Augustin as his training was to take so long (six years). In similar situations that we knew, families left behind reunited with the one abroad after a year or two. But I would say that was before the war: in normal situations.

So we were never successful in obtaining a visa to the States. One time, plane tickets had been bought but they were returned. After all, our country was at war. It was chaos. Nothing was going right.

CHAPTER EIGHT:
One presidential aircraft, hundreds of thousands dead…

In the Capital City as I rode the bus to work, I could hear people talking of war. There was fear among people. My days were almost the same: going to work, coming back home to my children. Despite all that had happened, I was grateful to be alive.

One morning in April 1994, I woke up to go to work. But there was nowhere to go. I heard on the radio that the plane that was carrying the Rwandan president and other dignitaries had been shot down, killing all the people on board. No one was supposed to leave his or her home. In fact, barriers had been put up overnight. What followed came to be known as "genocide."

It became clear that the war was at its highest point since 1990. The only sound to be heard was the sound of artillery. Bullets were flying everywhere like dandelions on a windy day! The babysitter at home had just taken one in her leg. She was bleeding right there in the living room. The bullet had come through the wall. No words could describe the feelings of fears of the moment. I could smell death. I could see it coming. I could almost touch it. The atrocities of the war were affecting the deepest nerve in my system. What was going to be our fate this time?

The twins' godmother, my very best friend in the world, informed me that they were going to the stadium nearby. I followed immediately. To get into the stadium was not easy. People climbed a tall brick wall. Children were thrown over the wall like bags of sand. There was no thinking here. Everything was moving very fast. What mattered was getting inside this place. I was able to get in safely.

The stadium, which was formally the headquarters for United Nations Peacekeepers, became a concentration camp for thousands of people searching for safety. No question, the living conditions were going to be hard. I stuck together with my friend and her family. But they missed their children. They had four children, but at this moment they only had one, the youngest. The others? They had a sleepover at a relative's in a different part of the capital city the previous night. And since barriers had been put up overnight and people were told to remain in their homes, some families were instantly separated. Were they going to be reunited with their children anytime soon? We only hoped they were still alive since people were dying everywhere.

After about two months inside the stadium, I learned that we were leaving in the night. It was then June 1994.

We walked out the stadium and headed north. The Capital City was in total darkness. Everywhere laid the dead. We were making our way through dead bodies; trying hard not to step on any of them. The smell was awful. No one was saying a word. We were taking it all in. It seemed we were meditating, quietly, silently and very sadly: An endless funeral procession! No doubt we were all suffering. To me, the end of the world in this small part of it, was no longer a myth...

Where was the moon?
Where were the stars?

Where was the light?
Where was hope?
Where was faith?
Where was the truth?
Where was the path?

So many questions but no answers. Only confusion, illusion, disappointment, fatigue, aching body, painful feet and a heavy heart.

We arrived at what used to be a sugar plant. We camped there for a couple of days and nights. We ate sugar and saved some for later. From there we had truck rides and we finally reached the destination. We were in the northern part of the country. We settled in what used to be a high school. It became a concentration camp for hundreds and hundreds of people.

It was a familiar place to me. I was back in my hometown. The same way I had left it. Back and forth, searching for safety. Hoping, surviving, breathing, struggling... This time I was not under the bed with the babies. And I was not hearing any sound of artillery. I would say this part of the country had been liberated. It had had its own share of battles back then. The major problem in the concentration camp was health....

I almost lost one of my twin daughters there. And to tell the truth, it would have been a very sudden death, even if we were all sort of half dead. The children were laying on a mat in a room. I was outside. My best friend who was in the room came to tell me my child was dying. I asked, "What?"

"Your child is dying," She said again.

I rushed into the room to find the girl's legs were rigid, stretched far out from her body. So were her arms. I touched them and they felt like hard wood. She was not breathing at all. She seemed to be gone...

I grabbed the four-year-old girl in my arms and started running fast, very fast and even faster. There were always endless lines of people waiting to see the doctor. But I was not going to stop in line. I simply couldn't stop running until I was right in front of the doctor's desk. He looked at me. I was breathing fast, almost sounding like a dog. He looked at my child. We did not know each other. There was no exchange of any words. The case spoke for itself.

It seemed there was no medication on the table for this case. The doctor disappeared in the room for a few seconds and came back with a medication that he injected into the child's arms. He told me to go back and lay her down and wait...

On my way back to the room, I was not running. I was exhausted. I was dragging myself and my child as well. She laid there on a mat and I sat next to her waiting for a miracle. The other siblings were looking on. No questions to ask. No comments. No words at all. This had become our way of life. Sometimes there is nothing to say. They just knew she was dead. They had seen so many dead bodies as we made our way through, walking.

After a while, my daughter seemed to be waking up a little bit. My friend told me it could have been a convulsion. I thought that was resurrection.

It would have been the worst of situations to live in concentration camps with no one close to me. As said by Baltazar Gracian, "True friendship multiplies the good in life and divides its evils/" I was fortunate to have this incredible family who stuck with me and basically considered my children as their own. They were the best people in the world.

Despite the poverty surrounding my childhood, I was happy. I did not have toys, nor nice clothes. I ate almost the same food at every meal, but I was happy. Even as a teen in boarding school, I was often asked if I ever got angry. Always friendly, smiling, happy…

But the faces of the war are pretty much the same:

> *Anger,*
> *Sadness,*
> *Loneliness,*
> *Pale skin,*
> *Dry, chapped lips,*
> *Teary, red eyes,*
> *Empty smiles,*
> *Yellow teeth,*
> *Runny noses,*
> *Bad hair…*

No one has the courage to smile. Everybody is hurting, suffering. If it's not physical, it's mental. It's psychological. It's social. Something is terribly missing. Something worth fighting for:

Peace.

A small wedding photo (1988) on Verediane's calendar quilt. *From far left:* Augustin, Verediane, her father-in-law and mother-in-law. The wreath around the image is handmade out of yarn.

CHAPTER NINE:
Away

The government forces were defeated. The Capital City was liberated. We could return to the Capital City. That was in September of 1994. Back and forth and back again. We had truck rides to the Capital City.

It certainly was sad to see what was left of this place. It was easy to find skulls, bones of what used to be a human body. The smell of decomposed bodies was extremely awful. The city was a complete ruin. Everything had been destroyed by the artillery. It was a real ghost town. It was definitely scary to be in a damaged house in which people or animals could come in from anywhere. No windows. No doors. But I liked to think that maybe, just maybe, the worst was over...

I had lost contact with Augustin ever since that April 1994. I did not have any means to communicate with him. He certainly followed news about his native country because what happened in this small part of the world became known all over the world. But Augustin knew nothing about us. Whether we were dead or alive, he knew nothing.

We depended on humanitarian aid. No food for children. No water to drink. No clothing. No jobs yet. Nothing. We were deprived of everything. Then one day, a nice lady I knew (we had been in the same concentration camps) came to my house. She claimed to have a visitor for me. I told her I did not need any visitors.

"If I tell you it's your husband, are you going to believe me?" She asked.

"Of course not! And besides, I don't want him to come," I replied.

There was nothing else to say. We simply stared at each other, as if we did not speak the same language. She seemed to be searching for some truths about what I had just said. Or maybe, she was trying to put herself in my position in order to understand my answers. After all, "You never really understand a person until you consider things from his point of view." (Harper Lee) I must have felt a little embarrassed and looked away…

Away, I saw two people coming in our direction. One was Augustin. Even as I saw him, I was still in doubt. After all, he resembles one of his brothers. As he got closer, I did not know what to think. I did not know what to say. I did not know what to do,. I don't think he knew better either. I simply cried:

> *Take me away,*
> *Take me away from anger*
> *Take me away from hunger*
> *Take me away from fear*
> *Take me away from despair.*
> > *I am thirsty*
> > *I am hungry*
> > *I am tired*
> > *I am naked*
> > *I am exhausted*
> > *Take me away.*
> *Take me away from hate*
> *Take me away from fate*

Take me away from evil
Take me away to heaven.
 I am frustrated
 I am disgusted
 I am confused
 I am humiliated
 I am traumatized
 Take me away.
Take me away from tears
Take me away from spears
Take me away from sins
Take me away from thorns.
 As sad as I am, take me away.
 As empty as I am, take me away.
 As small as I am, take me away.
 Take me away. Away. Away.

In Uganda, the children would be able to go to school. They would feel safer. They would play again. They would eventually heal and forget the horrors of the war. Augustin had only a few days to comfort them before returning to the States. Our oldest daughter was about five years old, the twins four.

Before "coming to the rescue," Augustin had raised money in the States, especially among NIU community, where he was a student. The money would serve us a great deal as we settled in Uganda. We were able to spend time with him in a nice hotel before finding an apartment. That was really a treat, considering how deprived we had been. Many thanks to those who were able to assist my husband in such time of crisis.

Once in Uganda, communication with Augustin became possible. We could talk on the phone, write letters and sometimes send a fax. The children made friends quickly and were able to play again. We had soap and water. We could finally take showers and rub some lotion on our dried skin. We had a place to sleep. We could breathe some fresh air and relax to music or read books. There was even television. But most importantly, there was food to eat and water to drink. We were alive!

I did not have a job there. Augustin provided for anything we needed. He would send money for school, for rent...

The native language of Uganda came fast for the girls. They were going to school and were taught in the native language with a little English. We lived in an open community and kids were always playing together; speaking the native language. Our own language was disappearing without us even realizing it.

Looking back, we might have lost our own language in our own country! After all, since April 1994, there was nothing to talk about, to children especially.

I think we simply looked at each other; with no words at all. The experiences spoke for themselves. They were very loud and clear. They were overwhelming. Sometimes there aren't even tears when you are hurt pretty bad. I don't think the girls bothered to ask for anything for which they knew I had no answers. We simply endured. We soaked it all in. With no words. It did not matter whether you were a child or a grown-up. And so, our own native language sort of became of no use for the children. It was lost; gone. Maybe forever...

Now, they were speaking the language of the country where there was something to talk about: food, friends, school, homework, shopping and so on...

Verediane's arrangement of flower petals.

CHAPTER TEN:
My cultural journey in America

"America, America,
God shed his Grace on me..."

The sound of fireworks on that Fourth of July 1996 was quite familiar to me. But these were bursts of celebration, not gunshots of war. After two years in Uganda, the girls and I were finally in the States.

> *It was a celebration time.*
> *A Celebration of life*
> *A Celebration of love*
> *A Celebration of peace*
> *A Celebration of family*
> *A Celebration of freedom.*

It was a celebration for America, "the land of the free and the home of the brave." It was a celebration for my family. We had just been reunited with Augustin. And since that Fourth of July 1996, the American holiday would carry a deeper meaning in my very personal life. Augustin's graduation was to follow in August. He was completing his doctorate program.

Our beginnings in the States were quite humbling. I did not speak

English. The girls had lost our native language. So, I found myself translating their desires to their father. The situation was not easy. It seemed there was no connection between father and daughters.

Upon arriving in the States, I met incredible people. Pastors John and Ruth Peterson became Grandpa and Grandma to our daughters. Debbie Coonley became Aunt Debbie. Mary Louis became Aunt Mary. I must say that a child does not call a grown-up by his or her name in my culture. So, it was by respect that these loving people were known as such in the lives of our children. They were special people to us. They had shown so much kindness to our family. We had nothing to offer in return. But as Armda Russel puts it: "Respect is one of the greatest gifts you can give to another human being."

The culture was definitely going to be something big in my new life. The fact that I did not speak English explains it all. I loved languages. I had graduated from college in my country with a bachelor's degree in French language and literature. I knew about five languages, but very little English.

Augustin did not have a job upon his graduation. We were on public aid, using food stamps to buy our groceries. That's when I found out I was pregnant.

I felt emotional thinking about abortion, something you don't talk about in the culture I grew up in. We lived in DeKalb, Illinois. We were sort of begging for food and here I was about two months pregnant. I was confused. I did not know what to do.

One day, Augustin and I went to DeKalb Pregnancy Crisis Center. The ladies there explained to us the procedure of abortion. It did not seem to be difficult, neither scary but for some reason I became very emotional, and found myself weeping, crying uncontrollably. When we left the office, I knew that abortion was not for me. I was going to keep my baby.

It was a normal pregnancy. No problem at all. But since the doctors did not have the record from the previous birth which happened by caesarean, it was going to be another operation. A beautiful baby girl was born November 17, 1997. She was named Grace Twagilimana. If the baby had been a boy, the name would have been Vincent, which means "invincible."

The meaning of a name in the culture I grew up in is quite remarkable. Each and everyone in our family has their very own last name. Here are the names and what they mean.

> Maliza: First born in the family.
>
> Zilikana: Remember.
>
> Tegura: Prepare for the future.
>
> Twagilimana: We are lucky. We have God.
>
> Mukagatanazi: Well made. Unbreakable.

We are not all the Twagilimanas, but we are one family. Grace is the only one to carry her dad's last name, because she was born in the States.

Indeed we are lucky. The day after Grace was born, Augustin got a job in Elgin (Illinois). He eventually worked two jobs to support the family. We were no longer on public aid.

Grace was about two months old when I fell very sick. I found myself crying often. I experienced fears that my baby could get hurt. Each time I held my baby, looking out the window, I feared she might fall through. And yet the windows were always locked even though we lived in a third floor apartment. What were these fears about? Was this post-partum depression? Were these fears from the time of war that had found a secure place in my memory box?

Nasal sprays did not help. It came to the point where I couldn't breathe through my nose. The doctor scheduled a surgery to be performed in my nose. The surgery and treatment meant I had to stop breastfeeding my baby for a whole week.

My culture had been of nursing mothers. Some nursed their babies for more than six years. My baby was only two months old. Was she going to understand why I stopped nursing her? And how if she refused to nurse after that period of a whole week? I was puzzled. I called the doctor's office and canceled the surgery appointment. I was going to endure the suffering but I was not going to let my baby feel rejected…

Augustin was working two jobs to support the family. He was leaving home in the night and coming back in the night. He seemed to be far out of reach for the girls, who would be sleeping by the time he got home. There was no doubt that the relationship between him and his daughters was going to be negatively affected; especially with the oldest who was lonely while the twins took care of each other, and remained inseparable.

With very little sleep or no sleep at all, Augustin dealt with stress by drinking every night. I found refuge and comfort in the Bible as I suffered from loneliness and depression. I was snoring in my sleep. I was sneezing whenever I opened the fridge. I thought I was terribly allergic to something and that something was alcohol.

For the first time in our marriage, Augustin and I experienced sex trouble. I experienced dryness which made love making painful. On the other hand, Augustin showed signs of impotence; which I believed was caused by the use of alcohol. In fact, alcohol had become his companion as we lived apart for so long.

We knew we were having deep issues. We did not talk about anything. In fact, we did not talk to each other at all. We were like strangers. It seemed we were somehow blind-folded; like a huge blanket was spread on top of us, a very dark cloud. We were on our separate ways, heading in two opposite directions.

In the midst of all that, I was considered the enemy—the person who brought the misery. I was the one who kept the children away from seeing and obeying their father. Never mind the six years, most of which they lived in the darkness of war away from him. Never mind that they did not speak the same language once reunited. So, there I was; standing right in the center, in the middle, blocking the view; stopping any connection between father and daughters...

I was carrying a heavy cross on my shoulders towards the mountain top where death penalty was waiting for me. It seemed divorce or even a miracle death would bring the two parties together. But make no mistakes: God is love. And God is the King of the living, not the King of the dead.

For sure, I was going to disappear. I was not going to sit in the driver's seat. I would not join on trips at all. I would not even attend graduations. And how about sleeping alone! I was going to go as far as I could, in the very back seat, but I was going to stick around for the sake of Grace. And from a distance, I would watch the twin girls fighting over the front seat, to be next to their father, as tears of joy filled up my eyes That's when I knew I was doing the right thing!

I urged Augustin to stop bringing alcohol at home. In fact, I wanted him to quit drinking. One day as I looked through the window of our apartment, I saw Augustin down below in the parking lot, drinking in the car. He was returning from work. When he got inside the apartment, I went to search the car and threw the rest of the alcohol in the garbage. I considered it was a family car, therefore, no alcohol in their either.

The next day after work, Augustin entered the apartment, holding a can of beer in the air as if to say: Now, what are you going to do about it? I looked at him and said repeatedly, "God is more powerful than the devil." I jumped up trying to grab the can of beer from him. The alcohol spilled all over me. Augustin then punched me on the mouth and one tooth fell instantly. There was a little blood on the floor. Also, Augustin took my Bible and destroyed it completely. It ended up in the garbage just like the alcohol drinks.

I called 9-1-1 from my next door neighbor and was taken by an ambulance to the hospital. I was released right away. There was no other injury except the lost tooth which I did not want to be replaced even if I could afford to do so. Augustin was in jail for three days on charges of domestic battery and before he could return home, we signed an agreement that he quit drinking and that I would do anything he would want me to do.

We eventually had a court case which dropped the charges of domestic battery. Augustin did stop bringing alcohol in the house but I wouldn't say he quit drinking. I might say it was going to be a long process. But I had made myself loud and clear on alcohol matters and I was never going to fight over it again. It was the only physical fight we had in our marriage. We had been married over twenty-five years.

We received counseling from our pastors John and Ruth Peterson. They were very supportive of our family. We love them so much. I learned that there is more than a romantic marriage. Any relationship goes through a certain kind of transformation. Somewhere, halfway, there is a new bridge to cross. And you are not safe until you have done so. Cross the bridge to finally be at the other side of it. Change is inevitable. And "The moment of change is the only poem" (Adrienne Rich).

Looking back at the experience, I can honestly say Augustin and I did not fight alone. Personally, I believe I was an instrument. I only obeyed. We had been faithful to one another. If somebody was to say, "How about the rape?" It was never an unfaithful act; and it will never, ever be... Augustin had come to rescue me and the children. In return, I had come to help him. Yes, I offered him alcohol whenever he came at my parents' home. In fact, I went oftentimes to buy alcohol for him if there was none at home. It was the culture. It was like following the rules, most of the time, blindly.

In our culture, alcohol was made in every household. There was alcohol made from bananas. There was alcohol made from sorghum. So, alcoholic drinks were ever present. They were the most recognized presents to deliver to friends and relatives. There was no age limit to who could or could not drink alcohol. Babies were breastfed but they were also given alcohol as well.

My mother told me that when I was a baby, she would put a drop of alcohol on my tongue for me to taste, and that I would cry all day! Then I told her that maybe I was drunk, to explain why I would cry. She said I never wanted it. She had realized I had avoided it altogether as I grew up. I might as well say, I was prepared, unknowingly, to answer the call when the time was right.

So, whatever the experience happened to be, sixteen years ago, I feel blessed. I am quite satisfied of what I did for my husband, for my family. Peace is worth fighting for. But to each, his own or her own way. Whatever you do for love, do it; not for power, but for love. "The supreme happiness of life is the conviction that we are loved." (Victor Hugo).

It was a miracle healing! No surgery was performed in my nose. I went on nursing my baby for four years. Not four months. Four years!

> *Faith is a personal matter*
> *As it is with love.*
> *Believe in what you know is true,*
> *Do what you think is right.*
> *Two plus two equals four.*
> *They will tell you it's five minus one*
> *Some will say it's twelve divided by three*
> *Others will admit it's three plus one*
> *Two plus two is equal to four…*

Where I grew up, religion was taught in the classroom. We memorized prayers, rosary. We participated in all religious rituals like the way of the cross and so on.

In this particular boarding school, we weren't even supposed to look at the boys while walking in line to church on Sundays. We looked right in front of us. There was a lot of discipline here. One girl was nicknamed "Virgin Mary", she seemed to be in prayer at all times. We prayed before and after every meal. We each owned a small New Testament. We were all about faith; whether we understood a thing or not.

It seemed we were all expected to be nuns. The letters I wrote to Augustin during that period of time started by "Dear brother." His to me were "Dear sister." Letters were read before they were given to us or sent to their destination. When Augustin accompanied me to retire my diploma, I introduced him to the principal and others as my "uncle". After all, how could they ever understand I had a boyfriend having just graduated from this particular school?

Upon arriving in the States, I was amazed at the availability of the book of God. A complete book. That's possibly the book in which I learned English the most. It became my companion whenever I felt lonely, which was very often. I even got to have a few ladies come in our apartment for bible study. I came to understand that "what you believe will depend very much on what you are." (Noah Porter). Faith is necessary to all of us. Without faith, there is fear. With fear, there is no freedom.

In any culture, it seems women are to look a certain way. But who is to define this certain way? I have been told that when you are a woman with short hair, you look like a man. And it seems to be a shame for a woman to look like a man! I have come to understand that it's okay for a woman to look like a man. I look like a man, and that man is my father! Aren't we all created in our father's image?

I wore pants for the first time while in the States. It felt right from the start. I could sit any way I wanted. I could put my feet up. I could move my legs freely. It was liberating. No wonder I looked up to my French teacher in high school, the first woman I saw in pants. Dresses are nice. Skirts are pretty. Pants? They offer comfort, free movement. They are nice, too. And for some cultures, they are a symbol of freedom for women who wear them.

We did not celebrate birthdays at all. In fact I joke with the girls that my parents may not know exactly the date of my birthday! After all, I was not born in a hospital and there was not calendar at home.

In the States, we have embraced the culture of celebration pretty well. Of course one step at a time, from just having a special fruit like "mango" to having a cake for dessert. We recently celebrated Augustin's birthday in a fancy restaurant. We have had birthday parties including sleepovers, especially for Grace.

I have been asked often what kind of food I ate back where I grew up. There was a little of everything. I would say it was the same food, maybe cooked differently. The weather was sort of like a perpetual spring, so food grew all year round. There was no weatherman; we listened to nature as she spoke her natural language. I saw snow the first time I came in the States. I find it is an accomplishment when I walk in the park on a below zero degree day!

CHAPTER ELEVEN:
You are not alone

The girls are encouraged to be creative as they grow up in a different culture than the one I grew up in. My wish for them is to have the best of both worlds. I am able to grow a vegetable garden each spring. I have had the girls shell peas and beans. They watch almost every vegetable grow: an experience I had myself as a kid.

We have embraced technology and I can see its impact on our lives, be it positive or negative. I am pleased to say it's been mostly positive. I believe there is hope for the future of our children. Growing up in a different culture may be difficult at times, but you are not alone…

When the moon is gone
And you are in a war zone
And tears are shed,
You are not alone.

When the stars refuse to show
And the wind starts to blow
And you are frightened,
You are not alone.

When the sky turns gray
And you can't afford to play
And you are worried,
You are not alone.

*When hope starts to evade
And loneliness to invade
And you think the end has come,
You are not alone.*

*When the path is bumpy
And you feel so grumpy
And you don't know what to do,
You are not alone.*

*When the earth starts to tremble
And the thunder begins to rumble,
And you think that you wan't make it,
You are not alone.*

*When bullets fly everywhere
And there's no safety anywhere
And you wish for better shelter,
You are not alone.*

*When truth is tortured
And love not so nurtured
And you think that's not fair,
You are not alone.*

*When your home is invaded
And your courage defeated
Because you are so defenseless,
You are not alone.*

*When food and water are scarce
And you see fear on your child's face
And you wish for a miracle to happen,
You are not alone.*

*When mortar and bombs are so loud
And the entire sky is such a dark cloud
And you think the heavens no longer exist
You are not alone.*

*When living conditions are so awful
And you have become quite so fearful,
Because danger is so omnipresent,
You are not alone.*

*When faith is forfeited
And hope is disputed
And you think that's not funny,
You are not alone.*

*When you've got those teary eyes
And you've lost all family ties
And you want nobody to see you,
You are not alone.*

*When harmony is silenced
And innocence is crucified
And you believe that should stop,
You are not alone.*

*When your love is so far away
And your peace is taken away
And you just can't take it alone,
You are not alone.*

*You are not alone in any circumstance.
You are not alone from dawn to sunset.
You are not alone in the darkness of night.
You've got to realize that mighty presence.*

"The circumstances of our lives have as much power as we choose to give them."

-David McNally

EPILOGUE

One way I learned English upon arriving in the States was memorizing quotes. I eventually used a needlepoint on fabric and had quotes displayed on every wall in the house. In the next few pages, there are some of my favorite quotes and how I relate to them.

"Walking is the best possible exercise. Habituate yourself to walk very far."
-Thomas Jefferson

Indeed walking is part of who I am. As a kid, I walked to every place: School, church, the market… I walked to the well to get water, to the woods to collect firewood.

My best memory of walking was walking with my father to one of the boarding schools I attended. We walked almost all day; and my father would carry the bag with my belongings in it. What amazed me was how long the walk was and I never got tired. It seemed my father rubbed his energy on me.

I felt protected, strong while walking with my father. I walked behind him, not by his side. One of his steps was two or three of mine. I was quite small compared to my father. I seemed to be jogging behind him while he walked in front of me. But there was no slowing down. Once we reached my school, he would walk back home by himself. It would be dark then, but he was powerful.

When I came in the States, we drove to every place. It took me a while, maybe two years, before engaging myself with what I grew up with: walking. It was not a popular thing to do then. In fact, someone wanted to know if I was okay since she saw me walking every day. I walk about three miles a day. That's probably not very far but I love it.

> *"The only real failure is not to learn."*
> *–Jimmy Carter*

I have failed countless times in my life. But I am mostly drawn to my secretary training…

The program normally lasted for three years. I only did two. And since I did not graduate from the program, you could say I failed.

Looking back, it was during this time I took an English class. In a country where only native language and French were spoken, I took an English language class. Did I know I would ever use it at all? But here I am in the States where I need it so much.

It also was the time I fell in love with poetry. In French class, we studied the poem "Le Lac" (The Lake). It was written by Alphonse de Lamartine, a French poet of the nineteenth century. I loved the rhythm and the rhymes of the poem. I loved how the poet expressed his feelings, his emotions, addressing himself to "the lake" as if it was a real person.

I learned there are no mistakes in poetry. You can't go wrong with poetry. You can even create new words. You can voluntarily misuse words, giving them a new meaning. In poetry,

> *You are the master.*
> *You are the maker.*
> *You are the potter.*
> *You are the creator.*

It's freedom of expression

In the States, two of my daughters have had Creative Communications Inc. publish their poems. The oldest daughter, Joy Maliza, had "No longer," a poem published in:

Celebrate!
Young Poets Speak Out
Summer 2005, p105

The youngest daughter, Grace Twagilimana, had "I will miss you," a poem she dedicated to her sisters as they headed out for college. It was published in:

Celebrating Poetry
Midwest- Spring 2006, p167

Another Grace's poem, "My Parallel World" was published in:

A Celebration of Poets
Midwest Grades 4-6
Fall 2008, p36

I met incredible people during the secretary program. I became a girl scout: an experience I enjoyed so much. I learned accounting and typing. I went to retreats. The retreat place was this quiet, isolated, breathtaking place with the view of the lake. We would spend a whole week in prayer, eating good food. I loved to see the lake. In fact, it was the very first time in my life I saw such a large body of water. I love the connection that water has with washing, cleaning. This was a moment of transformation for me.

So, I got what I needed from that program, but I was also needed somewhere else. The four year teaching program that followed meant more money than planned, but the training was extraordinary!

I might have felt sad about not finishing the secretary training but Jimmy Carter's assertion makes me feel positive about the experience.

"The capacity to care is the thing which gives life its deepest significance."
–Pablo Casals

Augustin showed so much care during the six years we lived apart. He seemed to be far and near. He seemed to be in both places at the same time! He came back to us three times. And each time, he had a caring mission to accomplish whether he had planned for it or not.

Even as we settled with him in the States, carrying with us mental and emotional wounds, Augustin proved he could put up with us. We might not have realized how much the experiences of horrors and fears we went through would affect our behaviors in the years that followed.

Augustin is a brave man. He has gone beyond cultural expectations in the care of his daughters. He has cooked a few meals for the family. He does laundry and cleaning by vacuuming in the house. He is involved with the litter box for the cat. Beyond all that, he has been the sole provider for our family for over twenty years! Augustin is a hero in every single way!

"The most powerful force on earth is love." Nelson Rockefeller

I am thinking about that moment Augustin and I were at Dekalb Pregnancy Crisis Center and the ladies were delivering information about abortion:

Why was I crying so hard?
Why were my emotions so high?
Why was I feeling so bad?
As if I was about to die!

Why was I feeling so small?
Why was I so embarrassed?
Why was I falling apart?
Like a forgotten dull doll!

Why was my heart broken?
Why was I so shaken?
Was abortion so forbidden?
That I had been insane?

Who was taking over me?
Who was defeating me?
Who was that powerful One,
To whom I surrendered, alone?

Grace, you are a miracle in my life. I loved you before you were born. I love you and I will always love you.

A family photo (2000): *Standing up in the back from left:* Sabine, Joy, and Sandrine. *Sitting:* Augustin and Verediane. *Front:* Grace.

Book Review of 'You Are Not Alone' by Verediane Mukagatanazi

PUBLISHED IN *THE PAPER*, SEPT. 3, 2014.

A few years ago, while walking around the park seeking solace from aggravations and challenges, I met the most cheerful woman I have ever encountered. She was smiling, striding out with confidence, head held high. I remarked on her cheerfulness, and convinced her to share lunch with me under the umbrellas in the courtyard of the Mansion. What was her secret? Maybe I could lighten up.

Turns out she'd been through hell, and come out the other side, though she didn't put it that way. ("When you're going through hell, keep going." -Winston Churchill.)

A native of Rwanda, a French teacher with three small children, she - and the children - survived genocide in that country in the '90's, and spent time as refugees before coming to this country. If you have ever seen the film, "Hotel Rwanda," available for rental from the local library, you will have some vague idea of the horrors that might entail.

Why was she so cheerful? "Because I'm **here**! And it's a beautiful day," she replied with a broad smile. All of which made **my** aggravations and challenges fairly inconsequential by comparison.

Verediane (pronounced Veh-reh-dee-ahn) has now written a book about her experiences. It is written in English, one of five languages she speaks, having learned the language of whatever country she was in as a refugee. In succinct, clear, and matter-of-fact style, she recounts a Rwandan childhood, growing up, young love, and passage into adulthood which despite the material and a few cultural differences, is not that foreign to our own. People are people everywhere on earth. The simplicity with which she documents her experience of genocidal warfare puts its terrors and horrors in stark relief.

In Verediane's region of the world, a child, at birth, is given a unique last name of his or her very own - not a patronymic - by her father. Verediane's father gave her the last name of Mukagatanazi. It means "unbreakable."

Good choice.

Cher Stallman

Stallman, Cher. "Book Review of 'You Are Not Alone'." *The Paper* [Dwight, IL] 3 September 2014, n. pag. Print.

www.ingramcontent.com/pod-product-compliance
Lightning Source LLC
Chambersburg PA
CBHW050041080526
44586CB00014B/1398